Tatjana Capuder Vidmar
Light in Architecture

Architecture | 101

Tatjana Capuder Vidmar is an architect and associate professor in the Department of Landscape Architecture at the Biotechnical Faculty, University of Ljubljana, where she teaches development of settlements, basics of architectural and urban design, and urban planning.

Tatjana Capuder Vidmar

Light in Architecture

Tectonic Relations Between Light and Shadows

[transcript]

The book was partially supported by the University of Ljubljana, Biotechnical Faculty, Department of Landscape Architecture.

UNIVERZA V LJUBLJANI | BF Biotehniška fakulteta

Bibliographic information published by the Deutsche Nationalbibliothek
The Deutsche Nationalbibliothek lists this publication in the Deutsche Nationalbibliografie; detailed bibliographic data are available online at https://dnb.dnb.de

transcript Verlag | Hermannstraße 26 | D-33602 Bielefeld | live@transcript-verlag.de

Cover concept: Kordula Röckenhaus
Printing: Druckhaus Bechstein GmbH, Wetzlar
https://doi.org/10.14361/9783839478660
Print-ISBN: 978-3-8376-8264-9 | PDF-ISBN: 978-3-8394-7866-0
ISSN of series: 2702-8070 | eISSN of series: 2702-8089

Printed on permanent acid-free text paper.

Contents

Acknowledgments

I feel deep gratitude for three great authors among many others. These three have expanded my understanding of architecture and the world: the Finnish architect Alvar Aalto; American psychoanalyst and Jungian student, Robert A. Johnson; and last and not least the Italian physicist Carlo Rovelli.

I saw Aalto's architecture one to one for the first time as a young student of architecture travelling one month by Interrail across Scandinavia. I visited all of the places with Aalto's architecture, studied the relation between the sites and the architecture, and explored the interiors of the buildings wherever this was possible. Maybe at that time I didn't understand his architectural theory, but his buildings in relation to nature, to urban places and landscapes, and to light, moved me deeply. Later, I saw a lot of world famous modern and contemporary architecture, but there were just few among them that moved me so deeply as he did with so many of his buildings. In this essay on light, I focus on his studio in Helsinki and try to show how he modulated the architecture with sunlight, as sunlight would be his chisel for sculpting the building. The architect's result of working with sunlight is an astonishing piece of art.

Aalto claimed that architects need to work for people and that we need to understand them when they are at their weakest. Why? I believe, the only reason is to empower people. Similarly, Robert A. Johnson empowers people with his many books. One of them is *Owning Your Own Shadow*. While I was interested in what light is and what impact it has on architecture, it became automatically obvious that I needed to consider shadows and darkness together with light. I already read the book before I had an exhibition of my works in February 2024 and titled it: SPACE = LIGHT (+ SHADOWS). It was one of the photographic exhibitions on my research of micro natural structures through the eyes of an architect. Which is to say, I have tried to understand the relations between volumes and voids of the micro structures. I observed them through a simple lens. The research revealed the beauty of relations between different layers and elements of the structures, and the beauty itself hidden in unusual proportions, a kind of universality on other scales, and that there were no symmetrical patterns in the observed structures. They cannot be observed without light and shadows. Even more, changing sunlight shows different relations between elements of the structures, and of course different shadows. According to Robert A. Johnson and Carlo Rovelli, we can pose the question: how big is the cloud of different possible relations between light and shadows in which we still find a balance – not only in natural structures, but also in architecture, urban design, and in landscape architecture.

Professor Rovelli most probably would not agree with the metaphoric equation I have used for the exhibition's title. I encountered the famous physicist for the first time in his interview for the Slovenian newspaper *Delo, Sobotna priloga* in September 2024. From the time I pursued my PhD and much later since 2010 when I started researching micro natural structures, interpreting them in paper models, I tried to understand what space is. Usually, we build architecture in space. But I think that a consideration that we should work with space not just in space is much more important than to simply build in space and ignore its existence. In the Rovelli interview, I liked so many thoughts he expressed. However, there was one sentence that attracted my attention the most. He said that in the smallest scale of observation, space shows a granular subatomic structure. I am probably one of many thankful readers of his books who enjoy reading them because we are mathematical amateurs and simple lovers of the magnificent universe. With the help of Rovelli, we understand a lot more than we did before. Through his books we can feel his enthusiasm for exploration of the world, its reality, and its beauty. We can imagine the complicated mathematical equations we have no ability to understand, and we can believe him when he talks about the beauty and simplicity of final formulas. Most of us are deeply thankful for giving us this knowledge in a simplified version that we can understand. So, I have found an answer to my two questions in his book *Reality Is Not What It Seems*. The questions what is space and what is light are probably the most difficult questions. Understanding the mathematical equations for both is absolutely beyond my abilities, but the professor's answer is simple: the reality of all things is relational. A physical system manifests itself only by interacting with another. What a relief for an architect! Architecture can therefore manifest itself only by interacting with another architecture, with an open urban space or landscape, but even more importantly, it can manifest itself only by interacting with space itself, and with light in the space.

August, 2025

Fig. i: paper model of micro natural structure and photo: Tatjana Capuder Vidmar

From the exhibition SPACE = LIGHT + (SHADDOW), DLUL, Ljubljana, 2024

Introduction

In everyday life light is something we take for granted. We know that after night, the next day comes with its daylight. The natural rhythm and relationship between light and darkness, between the scorching hot sun and dark summer shadows, between softer contrasts in all other seasons, between moonlight on the surface of water and darkness of the night, the relationship between sunlight in the crystals of a snowy landscape and its dark blue shadows, and between all colours and shadows in a landscape or a town during a day or a night, is not merely a constant occurrence day after day and night after night. The natural rhythm of light and darkness has a calming effect on us, and in relation with us it anchors us in space. Transitions create an awareness of the beginning and end of the day, crowning both with colourful shades of light and shadow across the entire visible spectrum. The transitions are slow – in a slow flow they build up the tension of a turning point, as darkness flows into light and light back into darkness. Our lives are more or less keeping pace with this rhythm without much questioning what is light.

What is light, anyway?

A quick look in some language dictionaries would tell us that there are two different explanations. One is scientific and explains the physical phenomena, the other is symbolic.

The scientific explanation is based on knowledge about the world. The question what light is, is perhaps as old as the oldest civilizations. In his *Theogony*, Hesiod[1], who was an approximate contemporary of Homer, claimed that cosmogony started with Chaos. Everything was already contained in Chaos, all the potentials and all of the archetypes for everything that constitutes the universe. From Chaos were born the personified darkness and night, named Erebos and Nyx. They became the parents of Aether (Ether) and Hemera, the bright sky and day. Light was conceived by darkness!

Isn't the Big Bang, an explosion in the midst of darkness, which happened 14 billion years ago as claimed by modern physics, a dramatic emergence of light in a way similar to the events in Greek cosmogony? Light dramatically broke out of darkness. In Hesiod's time, the event already lost its dramatic character and softened into personified siblings. Anyway, in ancient cosmology and in modern physics, light and darkness are intrinsically connected, though they are two opposites. In Hesiod's *Theogony*, they are entities with their own names and characteristics.

Modern science goes much deeper. Albert Einstein discovered that light is made up of small grains, particles of light, and he named them *photons*[2]. He also claimed that the energy of light is not continuously distributed in space. This was also later proven by quantum mechanics. A quantum field makes up light only in an

---

1 '[. . .] First there was Chaos, then broad-chested Gaia, the steadfast seat of all immortals who live upon the snowy peaks of Olympus, then murky Tartarus in the depths of the wide earth, and Eros, most beautiful of the immortal gods, who weakens the limbs and overwhelms the minds and wise counsel in the breasts of all gods and humans. Chaos gave birth to Erebus and black Nix, and from Nyx came Aether and Hemera, conceived after Nyx joined in love with Erebus. [. . .]' Hesiod, *Theogony*, https://ia803408.us.archive.org/14/items/hesiods-theogony-translated-by-michael-heumann/Hesiod's%20Theogony%20-%20Translated%20by%20Michael%20Heumann.pdf.

2 Rovelli, Carlo, *Reality Is Not What It Seems*, [*La realtà non è come ci appare*, Raffaello Cortina Editore SpA, 2014], UK, Penguin Random House, 2017, p. 92 – 94.

interaction. It is an event on a junction point of interaction where light is born. An interaction of two entities. Of Erebos and Nyx?

Rovelli, the new Hawking, as he was named by *The Times*, in his many books, but we will refer to the book, *Reality Is Not What It Seems*[3], luminously explains the contemporary scientific knowledge of modern physics. According to quantum mechanics, the events of nature are always interactions between physical systems. The world is made of quantum fields, so-called *covariant quantum fields*. All variable objects exist only in relation to other objects. Erebos and Nyx could be understood as two interacting fields, or two particles of the same field interacting with each other because, as Rovelli claims, reality is relational[4], that is to say, a physical system manifests itself only by interacting with another system. It is possible that this is true for all scales, very small and very large. The events are not predictable. They are undetermined. We can imagine undetermined processes and events in the midst of the ancient cosmogonic Chaos. It is possible that Erebos and Nyx met by chance or by their specific attraction. The regularities we see, as quantum physics proves, are ultimately statistical. But, Erebos and Nyx meeting each other or maybe colliding into each other, created Bright Sky and Day. Darkness and Night created Light.

Aether and Hemera are the result of the interaction of Erebos and Nyx. Quantum physics says that the world is a sequence of granular quantum events, which are individual interactions of one physical system with another. Light is formed by *quanta*, that is by parcels of energy of a field only when the granular structure of the field interacts! In other words, the light's properties manifest in granular manner only in the moment of interaction. Small grains, or particles of light named *photons* then exist in space. But, the most interesting is the fact that they do not follow

3 Rovelli, Carlo, *ibid.*

4 Rovelli Carlo, *ibid.*, p. 115.

a trajectory in space, but appear in a given place and at a given time only when colliding with something else. Light manifests itself only by interacting with something else.[5] We would have a black sky, as is the case on the moon if the sunlight doesn't hit the Earth's atmosphere.

The other understanding of light is symbolical. I assume that the symbolism of the Western world has roots in the classical Greek understanding of the world, which is expressed in Greek mythology. Greek cosmogony was a long and sometimes brutal process. It was Zeus, the son of Kronos, who seemingly created order after dramatic cosmic events. His Olympic family became a symbol for culture and civilization opposed to the previous barbarism and chaos. But even Zeus had his shadowy side. He was constantly cheating on his wife Hera. Leto, the goddess of motherhood, childbirth, and modesty, gave birth to his son Apollo.

Apollo became the god of wisdom and truth, of healing and prophecy, and he protected all nine Muses, and so he was also the god of poetry, music, and dance. He protected the human world from evil, and a bit later also became the god of Sun and Light, very similar to ancient Egyptian god Ra. Apollo was the most beautiful Olympic god and ideal *kuros*. Most probably the contemporary symbolism of light has roots in Apollo's characteristics and duties. Language dictionaries explain the metaphorical meaning of light as knowledge and victory over darkness, also connected to wisdom, truth, and beauty.

The etymologic aspect of light is also very interesting. The ancient Greek *λeukós* (white, blank, light, bright, clear) and *lúkē* (light, morning twilight), and Latin *lux* influenced Romanic and Germanic languages, and the word *light* in all its versions from *la lumière* to *luz, leggero, lys, ljus, licht*, etc. is metaphorically rooted in Apollo's characteristics. Meanwhile, the first syllable (sometimes the first two syllables) of almost all Slavic words for light (*svet-*,

5 Rovelli Carlo, *ibid.*, p. 117.

*svijet-, svět-, świat-*etc.) means *world*. The exception is Russian where the word for world is *МИР*, meaning in some other Slavic languages *peace*. In all Slavic languages, the same first syllable, sometimes with minor changes, also makes the word for *holy*.

This short analysis touches only European languages, as we presume that the Greek civilization is the cradle of the Western world. Still, there is no doubt that sunlight has meant survival for all known civilizations, and was metaphorically connected to everything that supports survival. In the case of the Western world, light is connected to wisdom, truth, health, culture, beauty, life in the world, and its holiness. It is connected to the basics which support human survival.

Darkness and shadow vs. light

Conversely, opposite to light but intrinsically connected to it, darkness is a synonym for death. It was the case in ancient Egypt and also ancient Greece. In Egypt, darkness is personified in Set, the murderer of his own brother Osiris, in Kek and Kekut, the couple of the principle of darkness, and in the belief that Sun dies behind the Western mountains every evening and goes into the underworld to be born again next morning. Ancient Greeks understood the underworld similarly. The Greek Hades, the god of death is the ruler of the underworld, which is named Hades after him. Metaphorically, darkness is a state of the atmosphere in the absence of light, connected to death. Symbolically it is a mental state of indecision and despair, and it is a state in which freedom, progress, and critical thinking are prevented or even forbidden, as we can read in language dictionaries.

Scientists already know some facts about *black holes*, but they admit that they don't know much about *dark matter*. It cannot be detected by the radiation it emits, but it has a gravitational effect on visible matter. And there is much more invisible, dark matter than visible matter.[6] That is why, despite the efforts of physicists, astrophysicists, and mathematicians to explain the universe, we are still left with uncertainties that challenge not only physics and other natural sciences, but also the humanities and arts.

Also, psychology and psychoanalysis have raised a question about darkness and shadow. They have found it in the human psyche. Robert A. Johnson, a disciple of Carl Gustav Jung, in his book *Owning Your Own Shadow*[7], tells us that the more prosperous a society is, the more shadow it produces. There is no light without darkness teaches Taoism.[8] Yet, as Johnson claims, the only solution for this drama is a cognition of the dark side. The cognition has a bouncing effect: in the moment of the cognition, we get "enlightened." The darkness fades away. Everyday life caught in all sorts of relationships, cast shadows. We might only find beauty in the cognition if these shadows become recognized despite the fact that they are causing drama or even because of it. Light creates the magic of the visible, but in such a way that the visible is only recognizable through shadows. It is not until the shadows become visible that everything that moves within, and the space around us becomes visible as well.

Reality is relational

However, light is just seemingly cut out of darkness. Evidently it emanates from its own source. This happens when the granular structure of the quantum field interacts and makes up light. Here we come back to the inspiring book of Rovelli[9]: *photons* are born

---

6 Rovelli, Carlo, *Sedem kratkih lekcij iz fizike* [*Sette brevi lezioni di fisica*, Milano, Adelphi edizioni s. p. a., 2014], Ljubljana, DMFA, 2016.

7 Johnson, Robert A., Owning Your Own Shadow, San Francisco, Harper San Francisco, [1991] 1993.

8 6th BCE, after Laozi, also known as Lao Tse or Lao Tzu, "the Old Master".

9 Rovelli, Carlo., *Reality Is Not What It Seems*, UK, Penguin Random House, 2017.

in the interactions. It is only in interactions that nature draws the world, as he says poetically, and also that there is no other reality except the one of the relations between physical systems. Reality is relational, and the relational aspect of it is universal. The world of existent things is only a realm of possible interactions between particles (or between fields). It is a sequence of granular quantum events. The events are individual interactions of one physical system with another. It is only in interaction that physical systems manifest themselves. Similarly, as electrons do not always exist, they exist only when they interact. In a moment of collision with something else they materialize in a place. And this event is not determined in advance. There is a cloud of possibilities of how it will take place and materialize.[10]

In this sense, we take a look at the interactions between light and physical objects. As Rovelli beautifully says, light arrives in the form of grains of energy, it has granular structure, and falls on a surface like a gentle hail shower.[11] What happens then, when it touches a surface? There is no usual answer. There is no predictable event. Nothing is determined. Each event is different, unique. This is also true for man-made objects, also for sculpture and architecture: two physical systems colliding and interacting, light and man-made surfaces. What happens in artwork depends on individual piece of art. In the relation between light and artwork, we get stories, great thoughts, and astonishing experiences. In this text, we observe four of them: László Moholy-Nagy's, *Das Lichtrequisit* (hereafter: the *Light-Space-Modulator)*, Daniel Libeskind's, *Der Holocaust Turm* (hereafter: *The Holocaust Tower)*, Senenmut's *Temple of Queen Hatshepsut*, and Aalto's, *Studio Aalto* in Helsinki. They are not depicted purely by chance. Observations are based on beautiful physical facts taken from Rovelli's book[12], as follows:

10 Rovelli, Carlo, *ibid.*, p. 161.

11 Rovelli, Carlo, *ibid.*, p. 95.

12 Rovelli, Carlo, *ibid.*

- Reality is relational. The relational aspect of it is universal.
- A physical system manifests itself only by interacting with another physical system. What happens then when it interacts with light?
- Light manifests itself only by interacting with something else. In this process, results are reciprocal. A manifestation of a physical system depends on another physical system when interacting and vice versa.
- There is a cloud of possibilities of how something will take place and materialize, how a collision of light and an object manifest a physical materialization of both, or a metaphorical story.

In the following text, I am inviting you to observe how light manifests itself while touching and interacting with surfaces of the artworks, while falling on a surface *like a gentle hail shower*, as Rovelli poetically says. We will also try to understand how the masterpieces manifest themselves when interacting with light, and what is the relation between light and the artwork. We need to be aware, as quantum physics proves, that for each solution in space there is a cloud of possibilities. Masterworks are materialized through an artist, through his or her ideas, thoughts, and emotions, and through his or her inner light and shadows, while dealing with the interaction of light and matter. Therefore, each piece of art is unique and unrepeatable. In analysing them, we will not be able to avoid to see the metaphorical meanings and the symbolic use of light while we are observing forms.

In Moholy-Nagy's *Light-Space-Modulator*, light interacts with the surfaces of moving sculpture. The result is moving photograms built up by moving shadows and moving cast and reflected light forms. It is a drama of seemingly playful shadows and light reminding us of everyday human shadows and also light moments that we create throughout our lives.

When there is too much shadow and darkness accumulated, and light is cut off in a society, we confront the dark side of the humankind, which is expressed in all kinds of aggression, wars, and other humiliations. Libeskind's *Holocaust Tower* is a timeless and universal symbol of the worst horrors which are still and again present in our contemporary time. It happens when darkness prevails and light is too weak. If in a society light in relation to darkness is too weak, we witness the most horrible evil we, human beings, are able to perform.

It seems the Egyptian Queen Hatshepsut was aware of how important light is, especially in the period of a year when it was diminishing. Through the magic in her temple, she performed light every year when sunlight was at the lowest point. The moments of magical light consoled her subjects and established her power at the same time.

However, in democratic societies we don't believe in artificial miracles. We do not need such populisms anymore. Aalto proved once again with his *Studio Aalto* in Helsinki that we architects can work with sunlight, that we can cooperate with it also in such a manner that sunlight and architecture manifest themselves together, and at the same time in the best possible form, in a certain place and time, for people. He has created architecture in relation to sunlight, place, nature, and people, considering that all the entities interact with each other. But in the case of *Studio Aalto*, it was mainly the relation to sunlight and the interaction with it that made the forms of the Aalto's masterpiece of art. It was through cooperation with sunlight that Aalto shaped the forms of his studio.

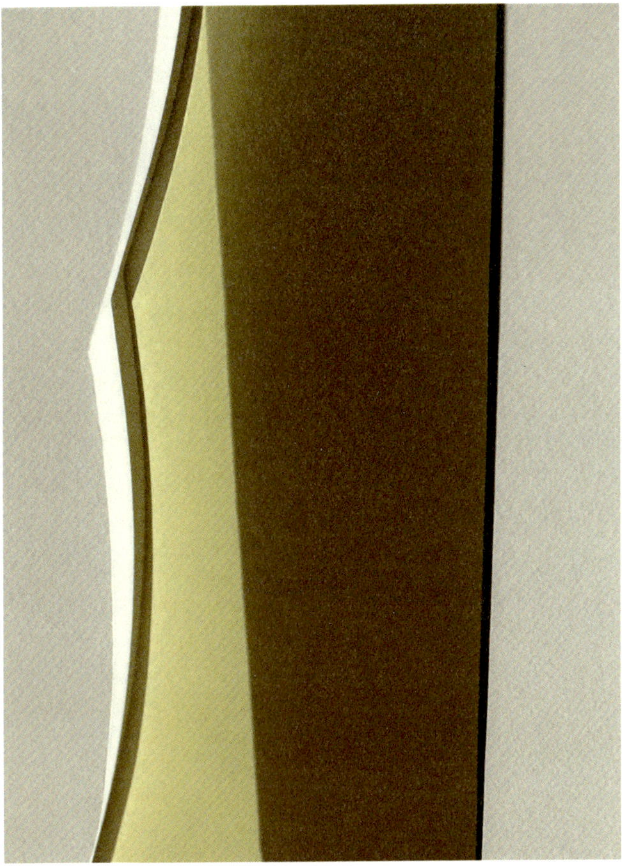

Fig. 1.1: paper model of micro natural structures and photo: Tatjana Capuder Vidmar

From the exhibition SPACE = LIGHT + (SHADDOW), DLUL, Ljubljana, 2024

Fig. 1.2: paper model of micro natural structures and photo: Tatjana Capuder Vidmar

From the exhibition SPACE = LIGHT + (SHADDOW), DLUL, Ljubljana, 2024

Fig. 1.3: paper model of micro natural structures and photo: Tatjana Capuder Vidmar

From the exhibition SPACE = LIGHT + (SHADDOW), DLUL, Ljubljana, 2024

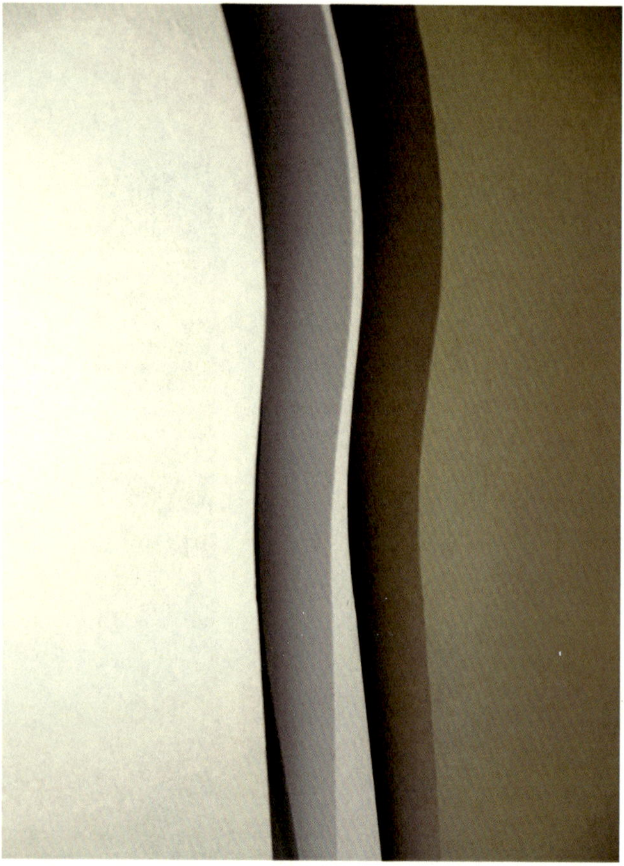

Fig. 1.4: paper model of micro natural structures and photo: Tatjana Capuder Vidmar

From the exhibition SPACE = LIGHT + (SHADDOW), DLUL, Ljubljana, 2024

Fig. 1.5: paper model of micro natural structures and photo: Tatjana Capuder Vidmar

From the exhibition SPACE = LIGHT + (SHADDOW), DLUL, Ljubljana, 2024

Fig. 1.6: paper model of micro natural structures and photo: Tatjana Capuder Vidmar

From the exhibition SPACE = LIGHT + (SHADDOW), DLUL, Ljubljana, 2024

Fig. 1.7: paper model of micro natural structures and photo: Tatjana Capuder Vidmar

From the exhibition SPACE = LIGHT + (SHADDOW), DLUL, Ljubljana, 2024

Fig. 1.8: paper model of micro natural structures and photo: Tatjana Capuder Vidmar

From the exhibition SPACE = LIGHT + (SHADDOW), DLUL, Ljubljana, 2024

1. An Interplay of Light and Shadow
László Moholy-Nagy, the *Light-Space-Modulator*, Werkbund exhibition, Paris, 1930

László Moholy-Nagy made his first drawing for the *Light-Space-Modulator* in 1922, after having moved to Berlin from Hungary in 1920, following his military service in Austro-Hungarian army in the First World War. In Berlin, he met the Dadaists and then Walter Gropius in 1922, and attended the first Congress of the Constructivists and Dadaists in Weimar in the same year. In 1923, he became a professor, first at the Bauhaus School in Weimar, where he took over the metallurgical workshop, a post he continued to hold after the Bauhaus moved to Dessau between 1925 and 1928.

It was a time of the re-evaluation of social values, promoted by art, and Moholy-Nagy's art was influenced by the following movements:

In Berlin, he encountered Dadaism. Dada in general was an artistic reaction to the tragedy of the First World War. The collapse of social values and norms that came with the conflict was countered by a free and irreverent art that ridiculed, insulted, and provoked the bourgeois society of the time. Berlin Dadaism understood artwork as political statements, and as a form of satire on contemporary established artistic practices.

Constructivism, an artistic and architectural movement, emerged in 1914 in Russia under the influence of various technological developments. It flourished after the October Revolution of late 1917, when the painter Kazimir Malevich first used the term *constructivist art* to describe the work of Alexander Mikhailovich Rodchenko. Naum Gabo then formally introduced constructivist art in his 1920 work, *The Realistic Manifesto,* where he with his brother Antoine Pevsner proclaims kinetic rhythms as essential forms of the perception of real time.

There was also an intersection between Constructivism and Futurism – the latter appeared in 1909 with Filippo Tommaso Marinetti's *The Manifesto of Futurism,* published in Paris. Both promoted a radical rejection of tradition (in both art and architecture) and a celebration of technological development and the industrialization of society – though constructivism was not interested in the other goals of Futurism, such as power, speed, movement, violence, and war.

There was also an influence from the architectural field. Between 1914 and 1915, Le Corbusier designed the Maison Dom-Ino, a modular skeletal reinforced concrete structure with open floor plans. He also published his manifesto "Five Points of Architecture" in the *L'Esprit Nouveau* art magazine, and in his book *Vers une architecture* in 1923.

In 1928, the last year of Moholy-Nagy's professorship at the Bauhaus School in Dessau, the 1st Congrès Internationaux d'Architecture Moderne (CIAM) was held at the Castle of La Sarraz in Switzerland. The 2nd CIAM Congress was held in Frankfurt am Main in 1929, where concern was expressed for the housing conditions of the general population, and in particular that of the working class. Moholy-Nagy attended the 4th CIAM Congress on the functional city in 1933.

Le Corbusier's architectural inventions have enabled a lot of sunlight to penetrate into buildings, as the suspended façades allowed wide, high, and long window surfaces, in contrast to traditional architecture, and especially the gloomy interiors of the speculatively built dwellings commissioned by industrialists for their workers during and after the Industrial Revolution.

The fascination with light was inevitable, especially since, as in the Enlightenment, it was a symbol of freedom, of humanistic values and of the fight against the dark conservative shackles of society, the petty bourgeoisie and against prejudice of all kinds.

In architecture, sunlight also had very pragmatic attributions: a lot of sunlight in a house meant healthy living in airy apartments.

In 1930, with the financial support of an electricity company in Berlin and the help of two specialists, an electrical engineer and a metallurgist, Moholy-Nagy managed to realize his 1922 idea for the *Light-Space-Modulator*. It was created at the intersection of Dadaism, Constructivism, Futurism, the goals of the CIAM congresses, and the general enthusiasm for technology, industrialization and, last but not least, light. It is a brilliant artistic upgrade of all these, but the artist also wanted to express his own view of technological development: "[the] reality of our century is technology: the invention, construction, and maintenance of machines. To be a user of machines is to be of the spirit of this century. It has replaced the transcendental spiritualism of past eras."[1]

This quote can be compared with Le Corbusier's famous statement that "a house is a machine for living in." Although he disagreed with the inhumane, capitalist use of technology, Moholy-Nagy believed that technology would improve life for humanity, and that art should be a prophet for this mission.

The *Light-Space-Modulator* was exhibited at the celebrated Werkbund Exhibition held in Grand Palais, Paris in 1930, and described as "a mechanism for generating special lighting and motion effects on a stage." At the exhibition, it was then placed in a box with an observation hole. The *Light-Space-Modulator* projected moving shadows in continuous motion as photograms on the walls of the box, which were generated in a sequence of preprogrammed light beams.

1 The source of this quote, including the translation, is "Constructivism and the proletariat" ("Konstruktivismus und Proletariat") by László Moholy-Nagy, first published in the Hungarian magazine MA in May 1922. Excerpts from the article were reprinted in the book *Experiment in Totality* published by his wife Sibyl Moholy-Nagy, New York: Harper & Brothers, 1950, p. 19.

Today, the *Light-Space-Modulator* is kept in the Busch-Reisinger Museum[2] at Harvard University, where it can be viewed without the box. It measures 151.1cm x 69.9cm x 69.9cm. The mechanism is powered by electricity via wheels connected to a bicycle chain. It is composed of high-gloss polished metal and glass parts. Frames with metal grids of varying densities are set on a circular moving panel. There are two vertical, shiny metallic circular panels of varying sizes perforated with small circles. There is a shiny black sphere trapped in a tapered circular and bent frame, along which the sphere slides as the frame changes inclination. The sphere is entrapped with a metallic sound for a moment each time when it slides to the end of the frame. There is also a smaller rotating circular panel with a metal rod with a spiral. This rod penetrates a hole in a glass plate, roughly shaped in a quarter of an ellipse. The form of the glass plate is reminiscent of the uterus – the skirt of the woman in Joan Miró's painting *Maternity*[3] from 1924, while the two perforated vertical circular plates of the *Light-Space-Modulator* represent the woman's breasts in the same painting.

The *Light-Space-Modulator* is a revolving world powered by the wheel of time, as hidden in a handcrafted Swiss watch. It moves the image of a flattened Earth in steady circles, just as we understood the universe in prehistoric times, when we believed that the Earth was flat and had defined and finite edges, and that this was all we had. Today we are aware that it has finite edges though it is not flattened, but we still know that this is all we have.

On a thin circular plate of the *Light-Space-Modulator* there appear to be a man and a woman with their reproductive organs: a spiral penis in the erect position penetrates the woman's womb, her breasts float above it, and an egg slides down the fallopian tube, cyclically maturing. Behind this archetypal image of a woman and a man rotating in their own rhythm, there are

2 https://harvardartmuseums.org/collections/object/299819

3 Joan Miró, Maternité / Maternity, 1924, Penrose Collection.

grids of different densities, coarser and finer. Each, in its tilted circulation, hovers precariously behind their backs, as a kind of explanation that they are being caught in the endless web of human relationships. It is only when this world is illuminated by the light of a soft sun-yellow classical bulb that the elements of this world become visible, precisely because of the shadows that are cast in this world and on the walls in the background in the form of photograms, as on a mirror of the world. The world in its rhythm and with the different rhythms of all the elements in it, illuminated by a static light source, is a polyphony that reveals in the images of the shadows the constantly changing interrelationships, each moment in a different position and yet linked into a harmonious whole and therefore beautiful.

Art of the highest order speaks to all the shades of humanity and the world we live in, says Robert A. Johnson in his book.[4] On the Busch-Reisinger and Getty websites we read that the *Light-Space-Modulator* is the most spectacular and complete realization of Moholy-Nagy's artistic philosophy, and that this piece is not only a mechanism for creating light effects, but also a sculptural object of beauty. It is one of the earliest light-kinetic works of art and plays a central role in the history of modern sculpture.

The interplay of light and shadow produced by the moving mechanism of the *Light-Space-Modulator* fascinated its author. On the occasion of the 1930 exhibition in Paris, Moholy-Nagy also presented his short film *Lichtspiel: Schwarz-Weiss-Grau*[5] to demonstrate the results of his sculpture. The rotating construction creates an astonishing array of visual effects. As it moves, illuminated, rays of light fall on the shiny metallic surfaces of the sculpture's individual elements. The light reflects from shiny surfaces and at the same time casts shadows on the elements of the sculpture and on the background walls. The interaction of

---

4 Johnson, Robert A., Owning Your Own Shadow, San Francisco, Harper San Francisco, [1991] 1993.

5 https://www.moma.org/collection/works/300671

light with the moving sculpture manifests the sculpture itself in many different perspectives by illuminating it. At the same time, light manifests moving photograms built up by different shapes of illuminated surfaces and shadows. The moving photograms together make a cloud of possible relations between light and shadow. Yet there are finite possibilities, all the time changing and at first sight, undetermined. The sculpture is a simplified version of human reality.

When we create light, we also create shadows. One cannot exist without the other. In the sixth century BCE Taoism understood life and its processes as a balance between opposites that are part of the same system, the Tao (or Dao). In the Tao, light and darkness need each other in order to be recognized, defined and understood – and thus they are needed for us to be able to understand the world and ourselves. The Tao is a creative synthesis of opposites.

If this is true, then it seems appropriate to comment the *Light-Space-Modulator* by paraphrasing Johnson. In *Owning Your Own Shadow*, he states that the creativity of a genious has the capacity to capture the beauty and darkness of the world in such a way that it is precisely through the shadows of the world that it creates and accentuates world's wholeness, which therefore becomes a full-blooded image of our humanity, thus – and only thus – approaching the sacredness of the world. In contrast to works of artistic genius, a one-sided interpretation of the world as good and bright is devoid of vitality or life.

Fig. 2: paper model of micro natural structure and photo: Tatjana Capuder Vidmar

From the exhibition SPACE = LIGHT + (SHADDOW), DLUL, Ljubljana, 2024

2. Facing the Shadow
Daniel Libeskind, *The Holocaust Tower, Jewish Museum*, Berlin, 2001

But Johnson states further that unhealthy societies might unconsciously accumulate a lot of shadow and manifest their unconsciously accumulated shadow layers in wars, violence, all sorts of neurotic behaviour, and man-made disasters. It is most necessary for societies and for individuals to confront the shadow layers in advance or at least afterwards. We need to pay off the shadows in an intelligent, symbolic way, which is, importantly, also through art, and thus become whole. A cognition is an absolute necessity, as claims Johnson, if the society or an individual wants to prosper in the future despite the tragic past. *The Holocaust Tower* in Berlin is an example of such a cognition.

The Jewish Museum has a staircase leading down to an underground level, and here three corridors await visitors. One leads to *The Holocaust Tower*. We walk along an underground corridor that is relatively light and airy, which makes the shock of entering through the black door into the tomb of humanity's greatest shadows all the greater. As we open the black door and enter the darkness, we become numb and breathless under the weight of the horror. I can think of no other architectural work which, with such a simple yet poetic architectural language as that used by Libeskind, shatters our very souls with such a force and then jolts us into cathartic reflection.

In 1993, Libeskind won the architectural competition for the Kreuzberg Museum in Berlin. The project is full of metaphor, infused into the dramatic nature of the building. As he explains in the film *Le Musée Juif de Berlin – Entre les lignes*[1] in 2002, his point of departure was the historical layer hidden a few centimetres below the then existing soil, claiming: "I happened to believe that space has its own authentic capacity."

The main entrance to the museum passes through the 18th-century Baroque building that once housed the Prussian Supreme Court. The friendly, soft Baroque architecture invites the visitor to enter in a deceptively innocent way. It stands on its own, separated from the new museum building, and they are only connected underground. The relationship between them is like a concealed monstrous violence. The façade of the Baroque building is like a mask of contemporary society, hiding terrible shadows in its depths. Just behind this mask, however, one must descend into the underworld. There we find *The Holocaust Tower,* one of the eight volumes that are like fragments of a straight line, which seemingly existed long ago in history. Now it is broken and transformed into disjointed line segments that are still trying to fit together.

These volumes are all empty, except for one, the *Void of Memory,* where flattened human skulls cut from iron plates are scattered on the floor and walking on them creates the eerie sound of chains on war prisoners.

The Holocaust Tower is "the voided void" and a relentless metaphor for all the genocides of the contemporary world. The architect managed to make the suffering of people visible and tangible through architecture. The tower is not part of the main titanium-zinc building of the museum, and its sole connection to it is underground. It stands alone next to the museum as a kind of splinter, a prehistoric unworked prismatic blade. Daylight enters the tower only through a narrow slit right next to the sharpest side of the blade, just below the tower's ceiling. From the outside,

---

1 Neumann, Stan and Copans, Richard, *Le Musée Juif de Berlin – Entre les lignes*, production: Les film d'ici, ArtebFrance, Centre Pompidou, 2002.

this slit looks like one of the scratches, wounds, and abrasions that appear on the museum's façade.

Inside, it forms a patch of light trapped in darkness high up under the ceiling. The light is weak, and because of its weakness it has no power to manifest itself. However, it manages to let us know that it is mundane, but unreachable. It is so far from us down there in the underworld that any hope of the freedom of the day is lost. This light accentuates our entrapment in darkness. It is a light that does not have enough power to illuminate the darkness in this endless abyss, because it is trapped in itself on the opposite wall of the tower. It is only the unattainable opposite of darkness. A powerless light that cannot be relied upon because it is too distant. Its presence only exposes the dark emptiness of the void. One would be hard pressed to find a more depressing atmosphere in any form of architecture, and this is precisely why *The Holocaust Tower* is a terrifying warning against the evil created by the hidden shadows of humanity.

Although the museum is a constant reminder that thousands of Berlin's Jews were deported and taken to Nazi concentration camps such as Buchenwald, Auschwitz, and Kaiserwald, it is also a mirror that faces all the political and military leaders involved in the more than 50 contemporary wars that nowadays destroy countries, causing genocide, and triggering the migration of millions of people all over the world. While I am writing, we have two major wars very close to Europe, in Ukraine and Gaza! In front of our eyes, through all the electronic media we witness genocide! The neurotic acts of war criminals who destroy buildings and entire cities, intimidate, humiliate, and manipulate people, deprive them of their dignity, their freedom of speech, their right to education and to express their culture, and destroy their lives mentally and physically, all justified by their ideology, their bigotry, their beliefs, and prejudices of all kinds, permeated with the lust to invade foreign populated lands, are the worst shadows of humankind, the darkness that humanity unfortunately produces over and over again. It blinds humanism, and is the opposite of the beauty of existence and the joy of life.

In the film,[2] Libeskind states that

> ... such a museum is necessary now [...] a story that will forever, eternally create a tension between the substance of the story what can be told and what can never be told, what can only be intuited and will always remain something that subverts any attempt to control and make the story fine.

Such an important mission of the museum goes beyond the horrors of the last world war and should be a firm and conscious warning against all contemporary wars. Aren't the goals of all wars very similar? Perhaps they differ only in the methods that try to achieve them.

With very simple architectural elements, Libeskind managed to show us what happens when metaphorical darkness prevails over light, when light is too weak or cut off in the relational interaction with darkness. Then it seems there is no cloud of possible results of the interaction. We get only one, finite and very determined solution: a succumbing to darkness in all its physical and metaphorical meaning, which is an act opposite to survival.

In his book, Johnson[3] put it:

> The tendency to see one's shadow "out there" in one's neighbour or in another race or culture is the most dangerous aspect of the modern psyche. It has created two devastating wars in this century and threatens the destruction of all the fine achievements of our modern world [...] Unless we do conscious work on it the shadow is almost always projected; that is, it is neatly laid on someone or something else so we do not have to take responsibility for it. This is the way things were done five hundred years ago, and most of us are still stuck in this

2 Neumann, Stan and Copans, Richard *ibid.*

3 Johnson, Robert A., *ibid.*, p. 27.

medieval consciousness […] It is a dark page in human history when people make others bear their shadow for them.

Fig. 3.1: paper model of micro natural structures and photo: Tatjana Capuder Vidmar

From the exhibition SPACE = LIGHT + (SHADDOW), DLUL, Ljubljana, 2024

Fig. 3.2: paper model of micro natural structures and photo: Tatjana Capuder Vidmar
From the exhibition SPACE = LIGHT + (SHADDOW), DLUL, Ljubljana, 2024

Fig. 3.3: paper model of micro natural structures and photo: Tatjana Capuder Vidmar
From the exhibition SPACE = LIGHT + (SHADDOW), DLUL, Ljubljana, 2024

3. Magic Light

Senenmut, *Temple of Queen Hatshepsut*, Deir el-Bahari, 1473 BCE

Queen Hatshepsut was obviously aware of the fact that when a society accumulates shadows without a timely cognition it might produce a drama or even a tragedy that could have a disastrous impact on the society itself and its survival. Intending to prevail her reign from potential destruction, Queen Hatshepsut introduced a special annual miracle in the sanctuary of her mortuary temple to neutralize the accumulated shadows of her subjects. The miracle occurred twice a year during winter when the sun was low and nights prolonged. That was during the time when people's survival was most uncertain. The miracle gave them hope for living by reassuring them that light was eternal and that the queen with the god Amun-Ra cared for them.

Queen Hatshepsut[1] was born in the 15th century BCE in the Middle Kingdom. She was the daughter of Pharaoh Thutmose I and his wife Ahmose, who ruled the 18th dynasty at the time. On her father's death, she was still a minor when she got married to her equally young half-brother, Thutmose II, who was the heir to the throne. Thutmose II died soon after, though, and thus she became regent to her stepson and nephew, the son of her husband and half-brother, the heir to the throne, Thutmose III, who was then only two years old. While not the first female leader in the history of ancient Egypt, she was certainly the most powerful, and ruled as the fifth pharaoh of the 18th dynasty in the following years. As depicted in a sculpture held at the

1 https://www.britannica.com/biography/Hatshepsut

Metropolitan Museum of Art (The Met, NY), she was a divinely beautiful young woman with a delicate, sweet face and large, almond-shaped eyes. She received all the same royal insignia as the male pharaohs did, with a *Khat* (a headdress), the traditional fake beard, and a *Shendyt*, a short skirt wrapped around her hips. Her status title was reinforced by the high priests with the story that Queen Hatshepsut had been assigned the role of pharaoh by the god Amun.

Amun, the "invisible," the god of air, was originally the local god of Thebes, the capital of the Middle Kingdom and later of the New Kingdom. By the time of the 12th dynasty, Thebes on the Nile had already become a religious centre. During the 18th dynasty, it took on a cosmopolitan image, but also reinforced its religious significance when Thutmose I commissioned a major extension to the Karnak Temple in Thebes. Later, during her reign, his daughter Queen Hatshepsut renovated the father's hypostyle hall, added a barque shrine, and introduced two pairs of pink granite obelisks. The original name of the temple was *Ipet-Isut*, because the temple stands on the ancient Egyptian *Chosen Place*, on a natural stone platform on the Nile, slightly raised above the river so that the area would not be flooded. The 18th dynasty dedicated it to the Theban Triad of Egyptian gods, consisting of Amun and Mut – the mother and the Earth goddess – and their son Khonsu. Amun was the most important of the three, and during the reign of Queen Hatshepsut he became the most important Egyptian god in general, the creator of souls and the god of fertility, the one who decided that she should become pharaoh. He merged with the sun god Ra to become Amun-Ra (also Amun-Re and Amen-Re). The largest area of the Karnak temple complex was dedicated to him. The main, longitudinal axis of the temple runs from the sanctuary of Amun-Ra in the east through the main hypostyle hall and three sets of pylons, and is perpendicular to the River Nile. It was additionally marked by the queen's two pink granite obelisks. It runs across the river, westwards.

The Egyptian hieroglyph for a town explains the ancient Egyptian understanding of their world. It was defined by two axes, the north-south axis, along which the River Nile flows, and – perpendicular to it – the east-west axis, along which travels the Sun. Both axes bring life. The Nile, with its annual flooding of the fertile plain along its banks, has provided water for agriculture for millennia, and the Sun, with each passing day, is the carrier of the light and warmth that all living things need. It rises every morning in the east and dies every evening in the west, plunging into the darkness of the underworld. The system goes around in circles, repeating itself day after day, night after night, year after year. And these years are counted in millennia. The eternal circle in which the two axes of the Egyptian world are caught.

The Nile divided Egypt into the right bank on the east side, where there were settlements for the living, and the left bank, where every evening the sun went underground, only to be reborn the next morning in the east. In the west was the city of the dead, and here is where the pharaohs were buried mummified to continue to look after the welfare of their country.

Queen Hatshepsut, the pharaoh, reigned for 21 years, from 1479 to 1458 BCE, during which time the country flourished, prospered, and achieved general peace. Thanks to the queen, Thebes' economy flourished as she renewed its trade networks, including those on the shores of the Red Sea. She also oversaw hundreds of large-scale construction projects in Upper and Lower Egypt. Among them were many temples, scattered throughout the country, dedicated to Amun-Ra, her spiritual father and partner, in order to consolidate her position as an equal to the gods.

Every year a multi-day celebration was held in the Middle Kingdom and beyond, in honour of the dead who lived in the Theban necropolis across the river below the western mountains. In a procession on the new moon of the second month of the harvest season of Shemu[2] Amun-Ra set out from the temple of Karnak, from his sanctuary, from where the sun rises, with his wife Mut and his son Khonsu in his sacred barque, through the hypostyle hall, along the axial path flanked by animal-headed sphinxes, to the river and across it on the central axis of the temple, westwards – into the world of the dead. The Theban necropolis was marked by the rocky hill of El Qurn, in ancient Egyptian Ta Dehent, 450 m high, with a summit in the shape of a pyramid. The Valley of the Kings is right below this peak.

Opposite the Temple of Karnak, on its axis perpendicular to the river, and in the distance to the west, just in front of the rocky ridge bordering the Valley of the Kings, Queen Hatshepsut built a mortuary temple for her immortal soul, as required by the tradition of the pharaohs.

And it was to this temple that Amun-Ra and his entourage set out from Karnak in a sacred barque every year on the new moon in the season of *Shemu*.

The queen began building her temple a few years after her inauguration, in 1473 BCE, dedicating it to the mighty creator god Amun-Ra. The temple became Djeser-Djeseru, the holiest of the holy, the home of the god Amun-Ra and the intended abode of the queen's soul after her death, when her soul would deservedly dwell beside Amun-Ra forever in the timeless future.

Centuries before Queen Hatshepsut, the ruler of the 11th dynasty, Pharaoh Mentuhotep II, was the first to build his mortuary temple on a mighty rectangular stone base, pushed to the foot of the cliff, right under the rocky ridge that borders the Valley of the Kings. Mentuhotep's temple was clearly the inspiration for Queen

2 Ancient Egyptians had three seasons: the *Akhet*, the time of the inundation, when heavy summer rains in the highlands of Ethiopia filled the Nile; the *Peret*, the time of sowing, which followed when the Nile receded from its flooded banks, leaving behind fertile land; and the *Shemu*, the time of harvest. Each season lasted four months.

Hatshepsut's even larger and more imposing temple, and was at the same time also her quarry.

The Queen's Temple consists of three high bases – the last, third base carries the whole mountain above it – and three terraces, the last two accessible by two long and wide ramps set on a central spatial east-west axis, starting in the east at the Amun-Ra sanctuary of the Karnak temple. The construction was probably supervised by the architect and high official Senenmut.

At the end of the central axis, on the far west and deep inside the mountain, there was a sanctuary dedicated to the god Amun-Ra and to Queen Hatshepsut. Amun-Ra sat there on his throne, waiting for his queen while she reigned.

He had also another important task. At the beginning of the *Peret* season, the sowing time, after the Nile had receded from its flooded banks and left behind fertile black earth, the sun began to slowly approach the winter solstice. Amun-Ra, responsible for fertile soil and abundant crops, and sunlight personified, would become illuminated in the depths of the dark sanctuary by the rays of the rising sun in order to encourage his people and alleviate their worries as to whether the seeds would germinate. In the second half of the sowing season, when the seeds had already sprouted, the rays of the rising sun once again shone on his image to make it clear to the people who it was that had enabled germination. In between these two miraculous events in the sanctuary of Queen Hatshepsut's mortuary temple, and precisely on the morning of the winter solstice, through the door openings of the pylons, the narrow rays of the rising sun illuminated the central axis of the Temple of Amun-Ra at Karnak and also the apparent axis to Queen Hatshepsut's temple. Who could thus not believe that Amun-Ra was the sun deity personified, providing light even when the nights were the longest?

The two wonders, which took place twice a year during the sowing season, were architecturally and astronomically planned with utmost precision. In mid-November and mid-February, the sun's rays entered the sacred space of Amun-Ra, deep in the depths of the cliff, along the central east-west axis of the temple, through two carefully planned yet hidden openings. First through the square opening above the entrance stone portal of the hall of Amun-Ra's barque, and then, at an angle to the sun, further on through an opening in the form of a horizontal narrow rectangle hidden above the stone portal of the Sculpture Hall. From there, rays in the form of a brilliant sun-yellow horizontal rectangle of light illuminated most probably the eyes of Amun-Ra. Each time the event lasted for about 10 days, when Amun-Ra gazed out of the darkness at his people with his shining eyes, letting them know, as a consolation, that the sun and he himself, the sunlight personified, were eternally recurring, even though the sun dies every day behind the mountains of the Theban necropolis and his strength was failing at the end of the harvest season.

Egyptian architecture – or what we know of it, the rest having been probably manly destroyed by the Nile inundations – is, like Moholy-Nagy's the *Light-Space-Modulator*, a dance of sharply delineated shadows and sunlight. The shadows are all the darker the sharper the sunlight. The colonnades of Queen Hatshepsut's temple cast black columns of shadows on the floor and on the walls of the colonnades. From morning to evening, they draw on the walls and on the floor the time of the sundial, which determines the daily routine of life.

But in the Amun-Ra sanctuary of Queen Hatshepsut's temple, something completely different happened twice a year, something that lifted everyday life out of the greyness of the mundane. The light of Amun-Ra's eyes was light in the midst of darkness, and not set in opposition to darkness. It was timeless and not spatial. The event in the sanctuary is a creative synthesis that glorifies the whole reality of the Egyptian world, showing that the glowing light in the midst of deep darkness is indestructible and eternal. It was the touch of sunlight rays in which Amun-Ra's eyes were manifested. In this moment, the divine light manifested itself. It was Amun-Ra's, the personified sunlight's manifestation. At the same time, the miraculous light manifesting itself, manifested the divine pharaoh's credibility. A simple but artificially dramatized interaction between God's eyes in the midst of darkness and sun rays caught in a rectangular shape manifested a confidence in the queen. Few moments twice a year were enough to convince and calm down the queen's subjects. A true miracle.

According to Johnson,[3] one does not stand such experiences for a long time precisely because they are timeless and spatially undefined. Yet, experiencing even just a moment of such an event is enough to give meaning back to everyday life, which is otherwise intertwined with a constant dance of light and visible (as well as invisible) shadows.

Queen Hatshepsut was obviously aware of this psychological need of her people. As Johnson argues, culture can only thrive if it realizes the unwanted layers of life symbolically.[4] Less healthy societies depend on unconscious shadow layers and manifest them, according to Johnson, in "[. . .] low grade ways of living out the shadow."[5]

Thutmose III, the stepson and nephew of Queen Hatshepsut, reacted in neurotic manner after her death. He was born heir to the throne, but he was only two years old when he should have taken it. Queen Hatshepsut was at first his regent. But then, by Amun-Ra's will, she became pharaoh in her own right and pushed the young Thutmose III into her shadow. When she died after having reigned for 21 years, the young heir was 23 years old. Judging by his actions, he could hardly wait to see the death of his stepmother and aunt. After the queen's death, Thutmose III had her images removed from the temple walls and replaced with his own. He went to great lengths to erase the collective memory of her, so that even Jean-François Champollion had difficulty understanding the hieroglyphs, as they spoke of a queen, while the reliefs and paintings spoke of Thutmose III. She was not buried in her mor-

3 Johnson, Robert A., *ibid.*, p. 48.

4 Johnson, Robert A., *ibid.*, p. 52.

5 Johnson, Robert A., *ibid.*, p. 53.

tuary temple, which she built for herself and for Amun-Ra, but in the tomb of her father, Thutmose I. His remains were moved elsewhere, and Queen Hatshepsut was placed in his tomb, which was dug deep in the eastern rock ridge above the Valley of the Kings, virtually behind the back of the sanctuary of Queen Hatshepsut's temple, behind Amun-Ra's back, and almost on the central east-west axis leading there from Amun-Ra's temple at Karnak. Down a 200 m ramp, deep in the heart of the mountain, Queen Hatshepsut is buried in a tomb marked KV20.[6] It seems that darkness finally prevailed despite of the annually induced miracles in the Amun-Ra's sanctuary of the Queen Hatshepsut's temple.

6 Queen Hatshepsut's tomb was visited by Napoleon Bonaparte in 1799. The marker system for open tombs was introduced by John Gardner Wilkinson in 1821, KV20 meaning King's Valley tomb number 20. By coincidence a motet by W.A. Mozart is also marked KV20 by Ludwig Ritter von Köchel (Köchel-Verzeichnis, 1863).

Fig. 4.1: paper model of micro natural structures and photo: Tatjana Capuder Vidmar

From the exhibition SPACE = LIGHT + (SHADDOW), DLUL, Ljubljana, 2024

Fig. 4.2: paper model of micro natural structures and photo: Tatjana Capuder Vidmar

From the exhibition SPACE = LIGHT + (SHADDOW), DLUL, Ljubljana, 2024

Fig. 4.3: paper model of micro natural structures and photo: Tatjana Capuder Vidmar

From the exhibition SPACE = LIGHT + (SHADDOW), DLUL, Ljubljana, 2024

4. Reconciliation Between the Opposites

Alvar Aalto, *Studio Aalto*, Munkkiniemi, Helsinki, 1955

The shadows, according to Robert A. Johnson, can be lived out and the wholeness can be created also by arts, therefore by architecture, as well. Architecture as a rule celebrates the beauty of living. Time and again, beauty of living is a primary goal of architecture. But if we follow Johnson's idea, we could say that architecture supports and celebrates life when it captures light together with its beauty and dark heaviness of the world, and with their interaction creates and accentuates world's wholeness. Aalto similarly claimed that:

> Whatever our task, large or small, starting from day-to-day ugliness, or the most sensitive emotional element, a town or part of it, a building, a traffic network, or then a painting or sculpture or everyday object, there is one absolutely vital condition that must exist for its creation before it can take on the significance that makes it culture. [. . .] In each and every case, there must be a simultaneous reconciliation of opposites.[1]

Aalto's statement was also proved by Johnson saying that "[. . .] personal effectiveness consists in standing at the centre of the seesaw and producing only that which can be counterweighted with its opposite. This is far from the sentimental view of goodness that has been set up as our ideal."[2] All of nature lives in

1 Ruusuvuori, Aarno, edit., *Alvar Aalto 1898–1976*, Helsinki, The Museum of Finnish Architecture, 1985, p. 39.

2 Johnson, Robert A., *ibid.*, p. 14.

polarities – light and dark, creation and destruction, above and below, male and female. As Johnson puts it, it is not surprising that the same law applies to our psychological structure. The balance between light and darkness is possible and even necessary to achieve, for otherwise the psychological shadows pursue us in the form of a mirror image.[3] This is where modern society has its problems, probably since the Enlightenment, when light finally theoretically triumphed over the darkness of the medieval social structure, and all collective darkness, as well as all the darkness of individuals, was pushed into the unconscious realm of the collective and individual shadows of the psyche.

In contrast, all great works of art give us a synthesis of opposites when they manage to balance the beauty and horror of human existence. They remind us again and again, even by surprise or shock, that there is a connection between things and concepts that we have always thought of as opposites. As Johnson noted in the same book, the geometric intersection of two circles, or the *mandorla*, is a metaphor for the intertwining of two opposites. But, when the synthesis of the two opposites is achieved, their intersection is not a space of neutrality or compromise. On the contrary, synthesis of two opposites, we might say, synthesis of two different fields, is an event of interaction and creation.

When light and darkness are no longer in an antagonistic relationship, when a spontaneous reconciliation is achieved between them, light and darkness can touch and create a kind of spatial miracle that appeases us, inspires hope and gives us the hospitality needed to feel at home in such a space.

To achieve the wholeness, Aalto used his own architectural language. His architecture is full of light, warmth, peace, amiability, and hospitality. It is a serene ode to everyday human life and gives hope that life is worth the beauty of being. At the same time, it is obvious that in his architecture, especially built

3 Johnson, Robert A., *ibid.*, p. 15.

in Finland, he was aware that light needs a drop of darkness as a contrast to light, to create an ambient as a wholeness of space. This is also proved by his Helsinki studio. In his architecture, he used only natural materials and worked with their own textures and colours, but additionally, as he said, he used only two colours: white and black, a lot of white and a bit of black, two opposites to be reconciled.

Alvar Aalto's architectural views

Architecture is part of the physical world, and is therefore confronted with a multitude of contradictions or opposites that only human will can capture, reconcile and transform into harmony through art. Even the technical and mechanical elements of architecture must be subject to art, as Aalto noted: "A harmonious result cannot be achieved through calculations, statistics, or probability calculations." and "[...], the main duty of the architect is to humanize the machine age. However, this must be done without scorning form."[4] After the Second World War, Aalto warned that life without art becomes mechanized, and that every architectural problem is different, so the solution to the problems one faces cannot be stereotyped.[5]

Aalto's early architecture was influenced by the Swedish architect Gunnar Asplund, with his architectural works classified as Nordic Classicism. He was probably also influenced by Le Corbusier and his five points of architectural innovation, which, among other things, advocated large openings in façades, thus allowing sunlight to penetrate the interior of the buildings. Large windows also enabled views to the nature outside. However, Aalto developed his own distinctive architectural form of expression. In fact, he categorically rejected any suggestion that he was influ-

4 Ruusuvuori, Aarno, *ibid.*, p. 156.

5 Ruusuvuori, Aarno, *ibid.*

enced in a conventional sense by other architects, least of all the modernists. He argued[6] that Le Corbusier's ideas reached him only through a general trend in the architectural discourse of the 1920s. In his later years, he even criticized Modernism. Very early on, in the 1930s, he had already observed modernist architecture with a degree of scorn, claiming that it was concerned with a world of forms based on the analyses of new materials, new building processes and new social conditions, but which simply created a mixture of chrome elements, large glass surfaces and cubist forms of unexpected colours, as if it were trying out all possibilities to become cheerful and obtain a human expression. But instead, it created, according to Aalto, the immediate and direct impression "[. . .] that it lacks the human element."[7] In his view, modernist architectural revolution had suffered the fate common to all revolutions: "It begins with enthusiasm and ends with some kind of dictatorship. It goes off the rails somewhere."[8]

After the Second World War, in the 1950s, Aalto also voiced sharp criticism of internationalism as something completely uprooted, claiming that the uniformity of internationalist architecture would not create culture in the noblest sense of the word. He was also critical of an economic policy advocating cheap solutions, stating that such an approach inevitably forgets the human, because it rejects a proportional relationship between quality and price. He added that when quality is neglected, the whole economy loses its sense in all areas, and architecture loses its sense, too. In the late 1950s, Aalto predicted a pessimistic future for Western European and international architecture, describing it as: "Parallelepipeds of expanses of glass and artificial materials – the inhuman dandified purism of our big cities – have produced a form of construction from which there is no

6 Ruusuvuori, Aarno, *ibid.* p. 13.

7 Ruusuvuori, Aarno, *ibid.* p. 147.

8 Ruusuvuori, Aarno, *ibid.* p. 147.

return – the road back is closed."[9] He also criticized the kind of housing construction that was carried out with a cacophony of motifs that do not resonate with the brilliant beauty of the variables in nature, of which man is a part. He was criticizing situations where man was forgotten. He claimed that architecture was a real thing that could be found only where tiny man with his tragedy or his comedy is at its centre. According to Aalto, an architectural solution must always have a human motive and this motive must become tangible in the construction. "Each solution is a compromise in one sense, which we can make most easily by studying man at his weakest."[10]

His architectural design also based on the classical architecture of ancient Greece and at the same time on the vitality of Italian medieval cities, characterized by a simple human scale, endless variations of the same architectural or urban motifs, the intermingling of public open spaces with private residential ones and, last but not least, the colourful bustle of life with a Mediterranean character.

As Kenneth Frampton said in an interview about Aalto for the Vitra Design Museum,[11] the Finnish architect also knew how to create interiors that made people feel safe and how to made them feel the warmth of being at home. For Frampton, the question of how to create a safe and warm home without becoming kitsch was crucial. In his view, Aalto could be a model for contemporary architects who seem to be completely unaware of this issue. At the same time, as Frampton comments the contemporary architecture, there is also the question of how to prevent it from being a cold, intellectual exercise, alienated from any human values. Humane architecture, such as Aalto's, deeply connected to nature and to human beings, is one way to approach this.

9 Ruusuvuori, Aarno, *ibid.* p. 148.

10 Ruusuvuori, Aarno, *ibid.* p. 49.

11 https://www.youtube.com/watch?v=SmBi_T-3ZAA

Aalto followed the sincerest humanistic motives. That is why his architectural designs are rooted in the emotional, mental, spiritual, and physical needs of people. But they are rooted as well in nature.

He believed that architecture with its details was part of biology, and should not be understood any differently from the way we understand biological phenomena. If this is not the case, architecture is not in harmony with the biological system of the whole, and therefore becomes inhuman. He was certain that architecture must always provide an organic link between the building and nature, of which human life is an integral part. In 1935, he had a lecture at the annual meeting of Swedish Crafts Association where he stated that:

> If we examine architecture in this way, that is, as part of the struggle between man and nature, we discover its clearest inner character, its systematic, constant variability. [. . .] The resultant 'natural variability of theme' is thus one of the profoundest basic characteristics of architecture, and it is of fundamental importance that we make room for it in our everyday work, too.[12]

After the Second World War, in 1949, he said that: "After all, nature is a symbol of freedom."[13]

Aalto rarely found inspiration for forms directly from nature, maybe only in details, which is, for example, how his famous glass vase was designed. It imitates the undulating shapes of Finnish lake shores and wind-swept water surfaces. His architecture in general was influenced by natural rhythms and textures, not pure forms. He used materials such as wood, white-washed or natural red brick, copper, and glass. All materials have their own innate structure and their own characteristics, which dictate their forms and functions. And while he never broke these laws, he explored

12 Ruusuvuori, Aarno, *ibid.* p. 33.

13 Ruusuvuori, Aarno, *ibid.* p. 34.

the limits of form in the use of particular materials. He felt that the miracle of natural forms and structures lies in their causality, and thus form is not just an empty idea, not an alluring visual image, but becomes a synthesis of reality. When this happens, form comes closer to man and begins to tell a story about the balanced forces in nature, one that it is up to man to hear and listen to.

Aalto's architectural, urban planning and design works demonstrate that his attitude towards nature was inherent in all his creative processes. Very importantly, he was able to preserve the original beauty of the landscapes and urban spaces in which he built his works. His buildings follow the natural logic of a given space and its characteristics, and support the beauty that had been present there even before construction began. His architecture repeatedly gives the impression of being an intrinsic part of a place, and of being completely fused with the spatial logic of a location, be it a landscape or a city quarter.

He did not follow modernist guidelines on how architecture should interact with nature. In Modernism, nature assumed the role of a kind of intermediary between man and his search for rudimentary sources, and also, as Le Corbusier foresaw, the role of a human measure. Anyway, there was no interaction with nature in modernistic approach on general. Nature became a romantic object of observation, admiration, and appeasement. In Aalto's architecture man is a part of nature, which is also an issue of Finnish traditional life. Traditional Finnish architecture is associated with hundreds of lakes and the timber of vast coniferous and birch forests, but also with the great seasonal sinusoids of changing sunlight and darkness. Traditional Finnish architecture contains traditional knowledge of man's connection with nature and survival.

Sensitivity to sunlight

While light is part of any architectural space, in Aalto's works we can recognize his outstanding sensitivity to it, especially to sunlight. Finland is a land where sunlight and darkness achieve a balance twice a year, and where summers, which have almost no night, alternate with winters, which bring bitter cold and darkness, in long wave-like rhythms. The Finnish winter is also a time when the very absence of sunlight makes us aware of its importance. There are countries where natural light is a given every day, but this is not the case in the far north and south of the globe. The long dark winters and bright days of summer create a contrast of sunlight and darkness, deeply rooted in the psyche of every Finn. Each year, from the equinoxes onwards, it is necessary to prepare for either prolonged sunlight or darkness, with the latter often leading to depression. But in the yearly reconciliation of darkness and sunlight, people's lives are nevertheless balanced when they can bask in the sun's rays.

Comparing to the long Nordic sinusoids of sunlight and darkness, much more frequent everyday rhythms and contrasts between light and darkness are caught in Moholy-Nagy's photograms of the *Light-Space-Modulator*. Anyway, the sculpture had an impact on Aalto's works. While he admired the Renaissance way of merging different arts, especially architecture, sculpture and painting, he saw the abstract art forms of the 20th century as providing strong support for modern architecture. The influence between abstract art and architecture was mutual and indirect.[14] In this sense, he was inspired by Moholy-Nagy's the *Light-Space-Modulator.* Aalto's inspiration drew from the Moholy-Nagy's sculpture resulted in architectural solutions for special illumination of interiors through ceiling openings. The skylights, inspired by the sculpture, in some Aalto's buildings are round as are round the penetrations of the two round metal plates in

14 Ruusuvuori, Aarno, *ibid.*

the *Light-Space-Modulator*, and they form a rectangular grid as do the holes in the metal plates of the sculpture. In Aalto's projects, the multi-faceted meaning of Moholy-Nagy's the *Light-Space-Modulator*, as explored earlier, has been given completely original and new layers of meaning. While the antagonism between light and darkness and the possible reconciliation between them in an ever-changing world is the subject of the *Light-Space-Modulator*, the interiors of Aalto's architecture transcend all opposites and transform them into a warm atmosphere of connectedness.

The round beams of natural light that pierce the dark ceilings in some of Aalto's buildings are functional, mostly illuminating rooms with diffused light, although rarely letting direct sunlight into the interior of the building. But they also have a symbolic meaning.

If we recall the analogy with Miró's painting *Maternity* and look at it on the other scale, then we can say that in Moholy-Nagy's photograms, the narrow cylinders of light, projected through two vertical perforated round plates are an act of giving light to a world of moving shadows, and thus symbolize the source of life. This is also true of Aalto's architecture. He consciously placed human life at the centre of his works, intertwining light into it.

In most of the central spaces of his public buildings, Aalto perforated the ceilings with natural light to create even illumination across the entire volume. Compared to, for example, Le Corbusier, who used flat roofs for outdoor living, socializing, sunbathing and recreation, or even for artistic creation, studios and kindergartens, Aalto turned his roofs into a fifth façade, letting natural light from the sky into the central halls. The library in Viipuri (Vyborg in present-day Russia) was the first of his buildings with a roof perforated with skylights.

The library was built between 1933 and 1935, a few years after Moholy-Nagy exhibited the *Light-Space-Modulator* in Paris. The ceiling of the library in Viipuri is Aalto's first architectural interpretation of the dark shadows projected on the wall, punctured in a rectangular grid by circles of yellow light in the *Light-Space-Modulator.* The effects created by the illuminated vertical perforated circular panels of the *Light-Space-Modulator* are similar to the effects of the ceiling of the Alvar Aalto library. The circular skylights pierce the shadowed ceiling in an equally regular, rectangular grid though in a bigger scale. Together with the ceiling, they create a play of contrasts between the dark ceiling surface and the circles of natural light. But in the library hall this play is transformed into diffuse light, diffused throughout the space so that all visitors to the library and the reading room can enjoy it.

It should be stressed that the even illumination of the hall from the ceiling is of course not accidental and, above all, is not merely a formal transposition of abstract art. Like the wooden corrugated ceiling of the adjacent reception hall, where he used the ceiling's undulating shape to ensure that the acoustics are even throughout the space, so that the speaker can be heard by everyone in the hall, no matter where they are in the room, he ensured that all visitors to the library and the reading room receive even illumination throughout the space.

The ceiling of the library in Viipuri is perforated with white painted concrete cones following the rhythm of a regular orthogonal grid. There are 57 of them, with a maximum diameter of 1.8 m. The depth of the cones is such that the sun, which in Finland shines at an angle of 52° or less, never shines directly into the room, but the sun's rays diffuse around the perimeter of the cones to create indirect lighting of the hall all year round. This achieves two pragmatic objectives. The books are protected from the direct sunlight, while at the same time the readers are not disturbed by the sharp contrasts between the sunrays and shadows that the sunrays would create. Each seat in the reading room is illuminated by diffused natural light entering through several cones at the same time.

Aalto used similar solutions for sunlight penetrating through the roofs of other buildings, including in the reading room of the Technical University of Otaniemi, in the central covered atrium of the National Pensions Institute in Helsinki, in Rautatalo commercial building in Helsinki, and in the library hall at Mount Angel Abbey in the United States.

For the illumination of his studio in Munkkiniemi, in the western part of Helsinki, however, he used sunlight in a specific way even more creatively.

The studio in Helsinki

The studio was built in 1955 and 1956, and is situated along Tiilimäki Street, on the granite hillside below, where the pink and smoothly rounded granite boulders seem to have sunk into the grassy surface long ago. On this descending slope a building is placed, bridging the incline and the ground floor so that the first floor, the studio part of the building, is almost at street level. The northeast façade is parallel to the street but not touching it, while a white brick fence runs parallel to the pavement. The fence creates an intimate distance between the studio and the street. The studio is seemingly trapped in an L-shape, which has its corner in the north beside the street and is completely open to the south. This makes full use of the site's natural light. Yet, the position of the northeast façade in parallel with the street is the only strict geometric regularity that connects with the urbanism of the surrounding villas. The studio does not interact with the street. The entrance to the building is on the ground floor, which can be reached from the street by a path leading down the granite bank. The building is introverted, facing the remains of the forest that grows over the bank. The south-facing L-shaped ground plan is softened by several irregular angles. The northwest façade, which could have formed a banal right angle with the northeast façade and therefore with the street, forms an angle with it that is a few degrees narrower, so that the façade is not perpendicular to the street, but slightly offset from the view from the street. The main entrance, which is on the ground floor of this façade and is reached from the street, is thus not immediately obvious. Aalto's studio is an introverted world, with its back turned away even from the perfectly quiet urban villa district of Helsinki, yet opening to the sunlight in the south and the trees that once formed a forest. In the surrounding space, there are also other individual houses set among these trees with all their ascetic grandeur.

Aalto made a peaceful environment in nature and silence for his studio colleagues, his wife, and himself to work in an atmosphere that allows contemplation, where one can immerse oneself in work without disturbance, and at the same time connect with creative collaborators.

The studio floor, which floats above the ground floor and the entrance, is one such peaceful environment. The ground floor consists of a reception office, a kind of filter that keeps the creative floor in peace. It also hosts a cloakroom with toilets and an entrance to the communal dining room with kitchen. The stairs lead from the ground floor to the studio floor at the point where the two wings of the L-shaped floor plan meet in the northern corner. At this junction of the two studio volumes, a meeting room is located. The two wings, with the studio drawing tables, have a different character.

The northwest volume is a trapezoidal prism with a sloped flat roof supported by visible concrete load-bearing beams, large windows to the northwest looking into the nearby treetops, and southwestern transom windows, which allow only view to the sky. These give the space the feel of a production hall, an office where architects once drew plans on tracing paper with pencils and ink, a parallel ruler, triangles, compasses, and other tools. The large transom windows as such do not open the view into the inner atrium between the two volumes, providing conditions for utmost focus to the ones making the project drawings. In this studio space, the drawing tables are arranged in strict order along the two parallel longitudinal walls. Some are separated from each other by wooden screens and have a more private atmosphere than others. Silence reigns in this studio space, and a rational discipline with an air of strict seriousness in the architectural design, even though the tables are covered with plans and the auxiliary tables and shelves are littered with various samples of bricks and façade ceramics, as well as architectural models.

In contrast to the northwest volume described above, the northeast volume of the studio is softly and organically designed. Even when designing his own studio, he adhered to his principle that every work should be a reconciliation of two opposites. The studio is thus a synthesis of rigorous seriousness and discipline and a soft, gentle and playful tranquillity.

The two volumes form a south-facing atrium. The atrium, opened to the south, there meets the old, mighty trees. This is not an ordinary atrium of an atrium house. Aalto turned the natural granite and grassy slope into an amphitheatre, an open meeting space where the roof is the sky, just as in ancient Greece. It is formed by a series of stairs descending in a loose quarter-circle. The wide stairs which also serve as the seats are made of stone, while the depth of the treads is covered with grass. The amphitheatre faces the white wall, the *skēnē,* which encloses the atrium to the southwest and stands in front of the *orchestra*. The white wall was used for projecting films on a large screen, and also played an important role in illuminating the interior of the soft volume.

In the atrium an echo of ancient Greek architecture appears once more. The upper ledge of the amphitheatre is embraced by the concave façade of the northeast volume. As the flat roof of this volume slopes down from east to west, the concave form of the façade resembles a large, high sail at full wind with its top pinned to the sky. This sail does not catch the wind, however, but sun-light. The sun's rays are diffusely reflected from the whiteness of the façade above the large windows at the bottom of the sail, and when they reach the south and west, they illuminate the interior of the northwest studio hall through the transom windows by reflection. Those sun's rays that fall straight through the windows at the bottom of the sail illuminate the interior of the soft northeast part of the studio directly.

This façade, this graceful, taut sail, draws the boundaries of the atrium with a form of an apparent mast in the sharp eastern corner but at the same time with its curve provides atrium's soft demarcation. The elegant white curve of the façade is set on a fluted base. It is like a lyrical motif in contrapuntal harmony with the *basso continuo* represented by the solid northwest atelier volume. The flutes are reminiscent of the flutes of ancient Greek columns and therefore of Greek architecture. They follow and support the long concave line of the façade. The flutes form the base on which the northeast volume of Aalto's studio stands. They soften the structural regularities with an undulating classical form that is rooted in the form of the mighty Doric columns.

The lyrical and elegant concave façade creates an inwardly convex wall of the northeast volume of the studio. The wall descends towards the entrance to the room. It has large windows above the parapet overlooking the descending bank of the amphitheatre and the *skēnē*, a white projection wall from which the rays of the morning sun reflect and illuminate the interior. Three drawing tables have been placed under the windows, which can already receive natural light at sunrise, even though they face south and west. They are illuminated by the sun's rays reflected off the white projection wall of the amphitheatre. And here begins the magic of the illumination.

Another large drawing table was placed not far from the east wall of the studio space. It was placed in the most secluded part of the room, far away from the main entrance. This is where the famous photo was taken in 1957,[15] of Aalto and his second wife Elisse sitting on Artek chairs designed by Aino Aalto, Aalto's first

15 Lukkarinen, Päivi and Pakoma Katarina, edit., *Alvar Aallon Ateljee 1954–55, Helsinki*, Jyväskylä & Helsinki, Kirjapaino Kari Ky, 2018, p. 46.

wife. The high eastern wall is perforated by large windows at the level of the treetops growing on the other side of the wall, a few metres away. The eastern sunlight penetrates the trees and enters the studio space above the drawing table. The green runner plant that grows up this wall towards the windows is seemingly intertwined with the treetops outside.

Behind this large drawing table and behind the backs of the chairs next to it is a separate high wall with one sloping side. This wall is cut into an upright trapezoidal form that largely extends upwards towards the ceiling. A closer look at the wall reveals that the reinforced concrete has been trapped in a formwork of thin slats, so that the corners of the wall are rounded and slightly displaced from a perfect line into an almost imperceptible dynamic shape. This wall has several functions. On one side, it delimits the space of the large table, on the other side hides the back door and exit from the studio. The back exit is reached by five organically shaped wooden steps. The door is small. It leads to an outdoor space under a low pergola. Similarly, the ceiling above the stairs in the vestibule in front of the back door is lowered to create an apparent porch of small dimensions. His effort to capture all the spaces, even the less important ones, in harmonious proportions is evident here, and to this end he sacrifices even the non-functionality of this ceiling of the vestibule. Looking from the studio space, this ceiling appears to be a balcony at the same time. It has a balustrade, but no door or steps leading to it.

The composition of the windows on the east wall is not arbitrary. It consists of a set of windows forming a vertical rectangle close to the convex wall and a string of windows forming a horizontal rectangle close to the trapezoidal wall. The two sets of windows are adjacent to each other and aligned with the top edge of the ceiling. The vertical rectangle becomes a square in perspective from below. It connects the windows at the bottom of the convex wall with the light of the horizontal row of windows. The peak of this spiral and from bottom up to the ceiling growing composition happens with the skylight just off the trapezoidal wall and at the same time above the large drawing table. The orchestration of the windows has built a harmonious light composition in which light from the sky descends in a spiral to the ground, and vice versa.

The skylight is the highlight of the magical lighting in the northeast studio space. The roof is pierced by a cylindrical opening which, in the passage through the reinforced concrete slab, becomes a triangular recess with one side longer than the other. The triangular prism hollowed out of the ceiling has all the inner edges and all three corners softly rounded. It is both sculptural and functional. It is designed to allow the slanting rays of the sun to penetrate the room and stop at the top of the trapezoidal wall. There, they draw a kind of a sundial. However, this sundial does not cast shadows and does not show hours and minutes. It shows the recurring cycle of the year. Strips of natural light are drawn on the wall, sometimes wider and sometimes narrower, depending on the angle of the sun, which changes during the course of the day and the seasons. The drawing of light formed in summer is thus very different from the drawing of light in winter. It is like the opposite of a photogram. It defines the time when it lets a piece of the sky into the studio space. The time of the sun and the Earth, and the time of the universe thus enter the studio and connect it to the infinity and the eternal rhythm outside. In the sanctuary of the Temple of Queen Hatshepsut something similar has been occurring twice a year, year after year, for millennia. Here in Aalto's studio, it happens every day, continuously, every day differently during the course of a year, and yet the same, year after year, in the eternal rhythm of life.

In his book *The Concept of Time*, Martin Heidegger[16] writes, "[. . .] every clock shows the time of being-with-one-another-in-the-world." Being with each other in the world – in the world of architecture – is at the heart of every architectural practice. There, time stands still in one seemingly infinite moment,

---

16 Heiddeger Martin, *The Concept of Time*, [*Der Begriff der Zeit*, Tübingen, Max Nemeyer Verlag, 1924], Oxford UK, Blackwell, 1992, p. 17.

which is the present. Immersed in architectural planning, the architect's every moment is in the present, even when they are working with their colleagues. The architect works on the basis of former experience and in-depth knowledge, but creation in the present moment is never a repetition of the past. In each present moment, which can last as long as needed, a new thought and therefore a new architectural form can be conceived, solving a current problem and not a past one. Creating in the specific present moment is imbued with an understanding of the future. If we take time in nature as our starting point, then the present already contains the past and the future. This is then *the extended present* Albert Einstein was talking about, isn't it?[17]

The rays of light entering through the skylight into Aalto's studio enter the space and draw on the wall the immeasurable time in which the creative work that gave rise to outstanding art was once immersed. Therefore, as Heidegger said, "[. . .] time itself is meaningless, it is transient and it is *principium individuationis*, a principle of individuation."[18] What matters is the visible result of an event in space and in an individual moment. There was light merging with space. In the interaction between light and space, nature, and people's need, an artwork was created through a sensitive and thoughtful artist.

Aalto's studio is a multidimensional spatial work of art, a masterpiece, and at the same time a state-of-the-art technical facility for passively catching natural light. It is the latter that governed the architectural forms, which the architect poetically integrated into a harmonious whole. Each architectural form was dictated by several relations and interactions at the same time. No form is a mere formal transposition of an imagination or a form transferred from elsewhere. Sunlight, nature, and man – and natural light and nature for man in a peaceful and

17 Rovelli, Carlo, *ibid.*, p. 52 – 60; on *extended present.*

18 Heiddeger Martin, *ibid.*, p. 21.

creative environment – were Aalto's obvious aims in designing his architectural work.

As was already explained, in addition to natural materials, he used only two colours in his interiors: black and white. The lightness of the light is grounded by shards of black. Large, bright, white rooms are furnished with wooden chairs with visible natural wood, upholstered in black leather.

Like Aalto's architecture, his interiors also reconcile opposites – including light and darkness. In the Helsinki studio, it is a fragment of defined black that transforms fields of light, which could seem otherwise metaphysical, into a real space. The amount of darkness in Aalto's architectural space is very small compared to the whiteness and light of the same space. It is as if it were in relative inverse proportion to the amount of *dark matter* and light in the universe.

Architecture is relational

Isn't the finding of quantum physics about inexistence of light until granular structure of a quantum field interacts, fascinating? If everything in the universe is relational, if the reality is relational, then architecture must be relational, too. If a system manifests itself only when interacting with another system, then architecture obviously depends on such interactions. As light, also architecture seems to be inexistant until it is in the relation to all related interactions. There are so many systems to consider. But if we follow Hesiod's *Theogony*, then it becomes obvious that there is a hierarchy in the creation of the world: the first entities created in Chaos were darkness, light and space. Time is only one of 12 Titans and was born much later. The modern physics was, as it seems, also occupied with light and space(-time) in the first place. Art usually follows contemporary scientific findings. It used to be so from ancient times to Renaissance and after till nowadays. There are also exceptions, that is great artists, who are even beyond the science because they understand the world with their creative insight and intuition even better, though they cannot prove it scientifically. I think Aalto was one of them.

But in general, it seems that nowadays the contemporary architecture does not follow the contemporary science. It seems it is stuck in the "dandified purism" as Aalto stated. Anyway, architecture can consider the basic entities and the interactions between each other, in the first place. That is to say, architecture can manifest itself in relation and interaction with sunlight – darkness and space – time in the first place and then parallel to these with many other systems where nature, human society, energy, and matter most probably prevail. What if architecture can manifest itself only in relation and interaction with sunlight and space in the first place and only parallel to that by interaction with nature and society, etc.? What if it cannot manifest itself if it doesn't interact with sunlight and space in the first place, and then synchronized by the interaction with nature and society at the same time? If not so, does it then become a lost opportunity floating in the space and being alienated from human society and nature, from urban tissue and landscape just because it did not interact with space and sunlight?

There are so many answers to what is relational in a creation of architecture. We have observed four possibilities *in relation to light*. Though the first artwork is not an architecture, sculptures use very similar language to communicate the relations between volumes and voids as architecture does. Moholy-Nagy's sculpture took individual human life interacting with endless web of human relationships. In the cross section between both the dynamic rhythms of the *Light-Space-Modulator* were created in relation to light. Libeskind's the *Holocaust Tower* challenges the weakness of sunlight in relation to heavy darkness in space. In this relation darkness manifests itself, while in the temple of Queen Hatshepsut sunlight overcomes the darkness and wins. It is Aalto who shows us the reconciliation of the opposites. And even more, his architecture is a resultant of many relations but the interaction with sunlight and space is in the first place and dedicated to people. His studio is a resultant of relations between darkness and sunlight, between sunlight and space, between sunlight and volumes, between volumes and voids interacting with sunlight, between nature and man, between man and sunlight, between man and space, and many others. This is why his architecture is deeply grounded into space and firmly connected to nature and people, and this is why it is never subordinated to the simplified Euclidian space. Because of all the interacting relations it is multi-layered and multidimensional, but despite of that it manages to reconcile all the opposites and be a harmonious whole.

Bibliography

Heiddeger Martin, *The Concept of Time*, [*Der Begriff der Zeit*, Tübingen, Max Nemeyer Verlag, 1924], Oxford UK, Blackwell, 1992.

Johnson, Robert A., Owning Your Own Shadow, San Francisco, Harper San Francisco, [1991] 1993.

Le Musée Juif de Berlin – Entre les lignes (Les film d'ici, ArtebFrance, Centre Pompidou, France 2002, Directors: Neumann, Stan and Copans, Richard).

Lukkarinen, Päivi and Pakoma Katarina, edit., *Alvar Aallon Ateljee 1954–55, Helsinki*, Jyväskylä & Helsinki, Kirjapaino Kari Ky, 2018.

Ruusuvuori, Aarno, edit., *Alvar Aalto 1898–1976*, Helsinki, The Museum of Finnish Architecture, 1985.

Rovelli, Carlo, *Reality Is Not What It Seems*, [*La realtà non è come ci appare*, Raffaello Cortina Editore SpA, 2014], UK, Penguin Random House, 2017.

Rovelli, Carlo, *Sedem kratkih lekcij iz fizike* [*Sette brevi lezioni di fisica*, Milano, Adelphi edizioni s. p. a., 2014], Ljubljana, DMFA, 2016.

Index